Handmade
Clear Stamped Cards

Barbara Gray

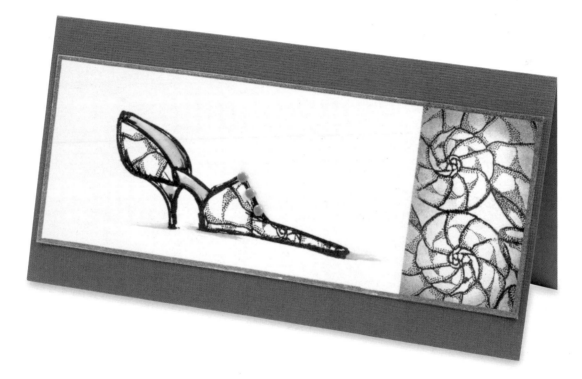

SEARCH PRESS

First published in Great Britain 2008

Search Press Limited
Wellwood, North Farm Road,
Tunbridge Wells, Kent TN2 3DR

Text copyright © Barbara Gray 2008

Photographs by Debbie Patterson at Search Press studios

Photographs and design copyright © Search Press Ltd 2007

ISBN-13: 978-1-84448-220-7

The Publishers and author can accept no responsibility for any
consequences arising from the information, advice or instructions
given in this publication.

Readers are permitted to reproduce any of the items in this book
for their personal use, or for the purposes of selling for charity, free
of charge and without the prior permission of the Publishers. Any
use of the items for commercial purposes is not permitted without
the prior permission of the Publishers.

Suppliers

If you have difficulty in obtaining any of the materials and
equipment mentioned in this book, then please visit the Search
Press website for details of suppliers: www.searchpress.com

All of the clear stamps used in this book are available from:
www.claritystamp.co.uk

Publishers note

All the step-by-step photographs in this book feature the
author, Barbara Gray, demonstrating how to make clear
stamped greetings cards. No models have been used.

Printed in Malaysia.

Dedication

This book is dedicated to my parents,
Hilma and John Gray.

Acknowledgements

Special thanks to Grace, Mark, Steve, Hayley,
Leigh and Dave, for being wonderful,
supportive and honest – always and in all ways.

Cover: Mail Art
*The layered effect is impossible to achieve with normal rubber
stamps, but clear stamps make it simple.*

Page 1: Purple Slipper
*The author's own stamp design, a simple sketched shoe, is
transformed by filling the space with the nautilus shell stamp.*

Contents

Introduction   4

Materials   6

Making cards   10

Victorian Lace   12

Fashion   18

Reflections   24

Mail Art   30

Two Tone   36

Grids   42

Index   48

Introduction

The art of stamping is, I am told, the most popular and fastest-growing pastime in the world of crafting. During the past twenty years, it has evolved into a sophisticated art form, and using clear stamps opens up countless creative doors, because you can see right through to the surface you are stamping on to align the images perfectly.

Over the years that I have been designing clear stamps, I have developed many ways to use them, and this book will explore a collection of my tips and techniques which can only be performed with clear stamps.

You can spend a mint on accessories and supplies (if you haven't already!), but all you really need is a stamp, an ink pad, some paper and a quiet half-hour to start. When you first begin, I recommend that you just try playing with your stamp. Try not to judge your first work against the projects in the book: I spent many hours on them, and that was after fifteen years of practice! Just relax and enjoy the art. Skill comes with experience, but fun can be had along the way.

I hope that the projects motivate you to your own works of art, and when you have mastered the techniques in this book, why not borrow one of my recipes and add some spice of your own?

Remember, it is about the journey, not the destination. Good luck!

Materials

When stamping, there are three basic materials: the stamp, the ink pad and the card. There are shops full of accessories and additional materials, but to begin with, keep it simple. Some basic equipment is listed here, but nothing too extravagant.

Clear stamps

Clear stamps are made from photopolymer, and are available in hundreds of different designs, from plants and animals to abstract designs and people.

There are many different companies that produce them nowadays, and as with all things, the quality varies.

Stamps can come mounted or unmounted. Unmounted stamps need to be attached to acrylic blocks.

The stamps used in this book are top-quality and permanently mounted on perspex. The blue colouring (known as indexing) is used to help identify the stamp when purchasing, and wipes off easily.

Ink pads

There are so many different types of ink pads available now, I could write a book on the subject of inks alone! Just remember this: <u>f</u>elt pads dry <u>f</u>ast and <u>s</u>ponge pads dry <u>s</u>lowly.

Also, bear in mind that archival permanent inks will stain your stamp and brayer: so always read what it says on the tin before you serve the soup!

A selection of ink pads and their effects. From left to right: black dye-based pad, peach chalk pad, plum archival pad, white pigment pad, dye-based 'cabin fever' rainbow pad.

Brayer

A brayer is a rubber roller. I use it mainly for background colour work, but it has many different uses that we will explore in the book.

Try to stick to dye-based ink when you use the brayer, as the other types will stain the rubber.

There are many brands of brayer on the market, but I would recommend a soft rubber roller, as this will give the best results when working with clear stamps.

Papers and card

Never underestimate the importance of the quality of cardstock you are using. There is a whole host of different papers and card on the market. When choosing card to stamp on, it is important that you consider the type of ink you will be using. Dye-based ink will soak into porous card, but will sit on coated (shiny) card. This can be used to give different effects, so it is worth experimenting on spare scraps before starting your final projects.

Pigment ink is oil-based, so it will sit on the surface of porous card, rather than soaking in. It does take a long time to dry, especially on shiny card, so always test first: you will soon see whether the ink and paper you are using are compatible.

As for background papers and layering card, there are wonderful plain, patterned, textured papers and card available. Pre-scored and pre-cut card blanks are also available, and these are fine to use depending on how handmade you want your cards to be.

Embellishments

The icing on the cake, the jewellery: I love embellishments! You can use brads, eyelets, feathers, beads, fibres, ribbon – in fact, anything that will add more flavour to the card. Embellishments always give depth to the artwork. Since cardwork is essentially two-dimensional, these bits and bobs give both colour and verve, and an important additional dimension.

Other materials

The following is a list of basic equipment I use when making cards.

Craft knife Used for cutting straight lines.

Transparent ruler with steel inlay This is an invaluable addition to any tool box.

Cutting mat Self-healing mats are ideal for cutting on, and are also a perfect flat surface for use when stamping.

Pencils Watercolour pencils are great because they change so dramatically when you add water.

Paintbrush It is worth investing in a decent fine sable brush, as picking nylon fibres off your artwork is not a rewarding way to spend your time!

Scrap paper This is mainly used for blotting and planning your work.

Removable masking tape This is used for borders and temporarily fixing items in place.

Double-sided sticky tape This is used for assembly work and layering the cards.

Sharp scissors These are used for making apertures and masks.

Deckle-edged scissors Decorative edges can be easily achieved with these craft scissors.

Gold leafing pen Edges can be finished with one of these pens.

Make-up sponges A make-up sponge can be used with ink to make a cloudy background effect on card.

Embossing powders These powders swell up slightly when heated, giving an embossed effect to your line art.

Heat gun A sound investment for any crafter, I use my heat gun for heating embossing powder and a hundred other things, too!

Wire The bead embellishments are secured to card with wire.

Wet wipes and kitchen paper These are used to keep the stamps and brayer clean while you work.

Making cards

The assembly of a handmade card really defines the quality of the work, and so we should strive for neat, sharp folds and cuts.

Over the years, I have developed my own method of making the basic cards, which I would like to share with you here. I usually work with an A4 sheet of coloured card and fit it to the artwork. That said, it is important to remember envelope sizes – otherwise you'll be making them too!

A4 is a good starting size, as you can easily make portrait (tall) or landscape (wide) cards. The key is in the fold: always work from the fold.

Note
This card was made using the masking technique on pages 19–20, and uses one of my favourite stamps: the shoe!

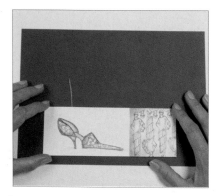

1 Take your finished artwork and place it on a larger piece of complementary-coloured card to establish where the fold will be.

2 Use a pencil to make the halfway line on the left-hand edge of the larger piece of card as shown.

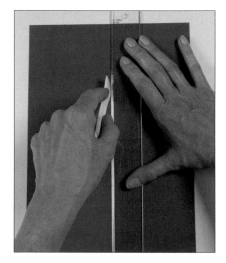

3 Repeat this on the other short edge, remove the artwork and carefully score between the marks.

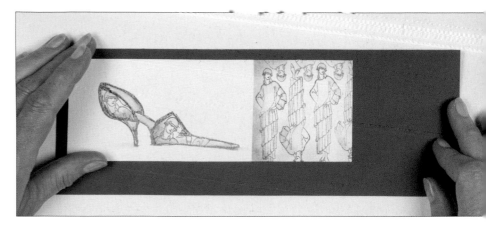

4 Fold the card along the scoreline. Always fold into the scoreline.

5 Use double-sided tape to secure the artwork to the card, aligning the top edge with the fold.

6 Use a craft knife and ruler to cut the other edges to size, matching the distance from the top edge to the fold.

The finished card.

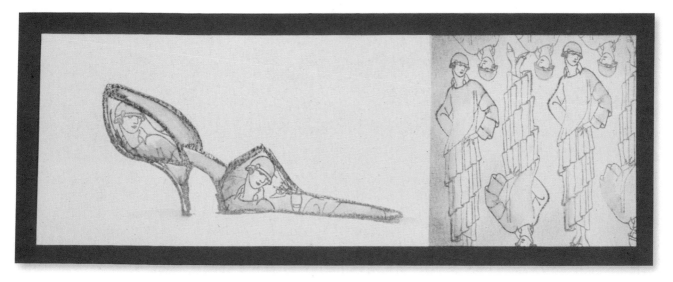

Victorian Lace

This card demonstrates the versatility of a little transparent corner stamp, which is used to create a repeating pattern and a seamless lace border. This sort of pattern-building is only possible with clear stamps.

1 Cut a 14 x 9 cm (5.5 x 3.5in) piece of watercolour paper. Ink up the rose stamp and stamp the image in the bottom left-hand corner.

2 Stamp the rose on to a sticky yellow note so the image is above the side with the adhesive.

3 Use the embroidery scissors to cut the outline of the rose out of the sticky note, then apply it over the image on the watercolour paper as a mask.

4 Run strips of masking tape along each edge, covering approximately 1cm (½in) of the paper on each side.

5 Ink the Victorian corner stamp and blot it until it is a little faded, then stamp over the masking tape, allowing only the very tip of the stamp to print on the paper. Repeat this action to the left so that the second impression touches the first.

You Will Need

Clear stamps: rose, Topaze, Victorian corner

A4 sheets of 300gsm (140lb) cold-pressed watercolour paper

A4 sheet of lilac textured paper

Scrap paper

Dye-based eggplant ink pad

Low-tack masking tape

Five small gold beads

Lilac bead

10cm (4in) cord

Craft knife and cutting mat

Ruler

Embroidery scissors

Lilac colouring pencil

1/16in hole punch

Gold leafing pen

Gold wire

Sticky foam pads

Large sticky yellow notes

Double-sided sticky tape

Tip

When pattern-building with corner stamps, always practise on scrap paper to get a feel for the little stamp before you begin.

6 Repeat all around the masking tape until you reach the start.

7 Run masking tape along the tips of the top border, then ink and blot the corner stamp. Stamp the tip into the spaces between the tips of the border.

8 Work along the row, stamping into each space, then remove the masking tape, being careful not to tear the rose mask.

9 Work around the other edges in the same way, then remove the masking tape and rose mask. Use a lilac colouring pencil to add a touch of colour to the rose.

10 Cut a 3¾ x 7½cm (1.5 x 3in) piece of watercolour paper, then trim the top corners off to make a tag (see inset). Ink the Topaze stamp and stamp the tag, then use the tip of the Victorian corner stamp to stamp a border as before.

11 Colour Topaze's clothing with the lilac colouring pencil, then attach the tag to lilac paper with double-sided tape.

12 Cut the tag out, leaving a thin border of lilac card. Punch a hole in the tag with the hole punch, thread the cord through the hole and then thread three beads (gold, lilac and gold) on to both ends of the cord.

13 Take a 5 x 12¾cm (2 x 5in) piece of watercolour paper and ink the corner stamp. Blot it and stamp the paper in the top right corner.

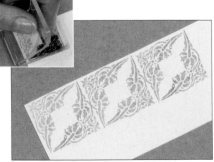

14 Turn the strip round, ink the stamp, blot it and stamp next to the previous impression, creating a square (see inset). Make two more squares adjacent to the first.

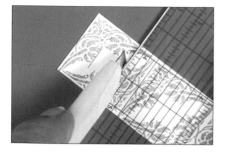

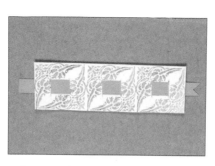

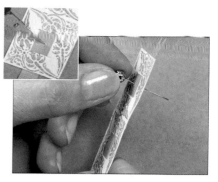

15 Use the craft knife to cut the motif out, then make a slit in the top and bottom part of the inside square of the designs as shown.

16 Cut a 0.75 x 14cm (¼ x 5½in) strip of lilac card and thread it through the slits. Make a swallow's-tail notch at one end.

17 Use the tip of your embroidery scissors to make a hole in the strip at the centre of each square (see inset). Thread a 7¾cm (3in) piece of gold wire with a bead, then poke both ends through the hole.

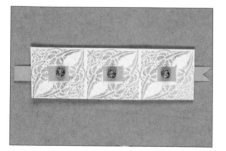

18 Twist the wire to secure the bead, and repeat the process on the other two holes.

19 Nuzzle the nib of the gold leafing pen on the edge of the motif and drag the pen along the side to edge it. Repeat the process on the main artwork.

20 Mount both pieces on lilac card (as in steps 11 and 12), then make a card from an A4 piece of watercolour paper and attach the pieces with double-sided sticky tape.

21 Attach the tag to the main artwork with sticky foam pads to complete the card.

Ornate Variations in Blue

This card illustrates several patterns using the same wonderful lace-making corner.

Three Honeysuckle Notelets

One small honeysuckle corner stamp; three delightful central motifs and a lovely border to link them to one another.

Catherine Wheel

Another variation using the Victorian corner. Here, the Catherine wheel actually rotates, turning on a brad.

Fashion

In this chapter, I want to show you how to completely alter a stamp by filling the image with another stamp – another technique that is only possible with a transparent stamp.

An ornate corner stamp is used again in this chapter to emphasise their flexibility.

YOU WILL NEED

Clear stamps: tailor's dummy, ornate corner

A4 sheets of 300gsm (140lb) cold-pressed watercolour paper

A4 brown card

Dye-based sepia archival ink pad

Dye-based currant ink pad

Make-up sponge

Gold leafing pen

Three brads

Embroidery scissors

Paintbrush

Large sticky yellow notes

Double-sided sticky tape

1 Use the tailor's dummy stamp with the sepia ink and stamp right in the centre of the 15 x 10cm (6 x 4in) piece of watercolour paper.

2 Stamp it again on a large sticky note and use a pair of embroidery scissors to cut out the body (not the stand) of the dummy to make a mask.

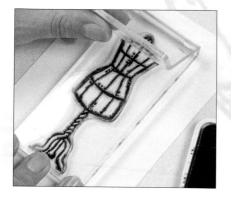

3 Position the mask over the impression on the watercolour paper and place other sticky notes over the rest of the paper to protect it. Ink the ornate corner stamp with sepia ink, blot it, then position the tip in the centre of the dummy's waist as shown to stamp the bottom left part of the dummy.

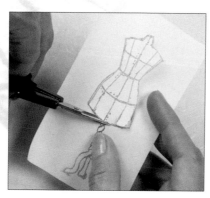

4 Ink and blot the stamp again, then turn the stamp through ninety degrees and stamp the tip in the centre to mark the bottom right part of the dummy.

5 Stamp the top corners in the same way to complete the pattern.

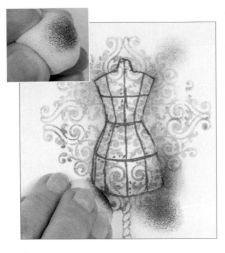

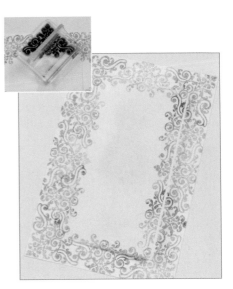

6 Pinch the corners of the make-up sponge in your fingers to force the centre out into a mushroom shape (see inset). Dab this into the currant ink, blot it on scrap paper and dab it gently round the edges of the tailor's dummy.

Tip
Build the colour up gradually with the sponge. You can add colour, but you can not take it away.

7 Peel off all of the sticky notes, then cover the dummy in the centre with a new note (see inset). Place the card on scrap paper and use the ornate corner stamp with sepia archival ink to stamp each of the corners and the two long edges. Remember to blot the stamp.

8 Ink blot and stamp the space between impressions, looking through the stamp to make sure that the pattern matches up well with the existing stamped impressions (see inset).

9 Use the make-up sponge with currant ink to gradually build up colour around the inside border.

10 Remove the large sticky note and use a damp paintbrush to pick up a little currant ink and paint the stand.

11 Push the nib of the gold leafing pen down on the side of the card and drag it all the way round to edge the card.

12 Use the point of your embroidery scissors to pierce the dummy where the seams cross the centre of the chest.

13 Push a brad through the hole and secure.

14 Repeat twice more to complete the artwork, then make a brown card and attach the artwork with double-sided sticky tape to finish the card.

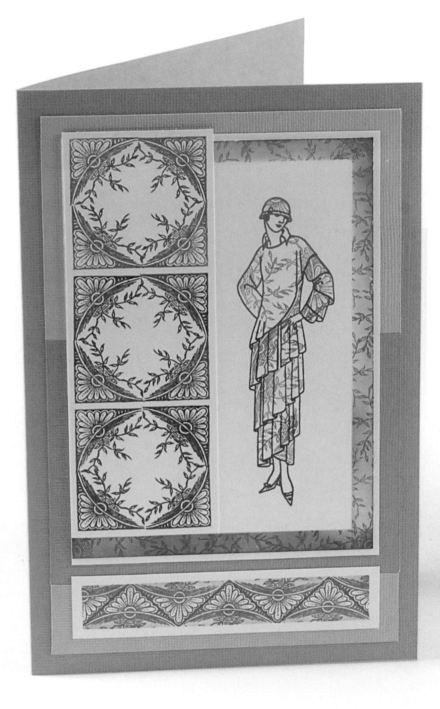

Kasha and the Leafy Corner

This entire card was created using just two stamps
(the lady and the leafy corner) and different parts of
a rainbow ink pad. Oh – and hours of focus and fun!

The Geisha in Love

The Geisha's dress is painted in folds, and only the folds are filled with the love symbol.

Paris in the Spring

The Parisian lady's dress is filled using the same honeysuckle stamp used on the notelets on pages 16–17.

Reflections

I developed the technique used here when working with a brayer. Everybody who has seen this card loves it, so this has become a favourite technique of mine. Rainbow pads work beautifully here. Never worry that a tree is not green or that the water may not be blue. This is artwork, not a photograph!

YOU WILL NEED

Clear stamps: daydreamer, grass, moonshadow

Dye-based stained glass rainbow ink pad

A4 dark blue card

A5 satin-finish white card

Scrap paper

Brayer

Large sticky yellow notes

Double-sided sticky tape

Craft knife, cutting mat and metal-edged ruler

1 Run masking tape round three sides of the satin-finish card, right to the edges. Run a fourth strip along the bottom edge, offset by 1½cm (¾in).

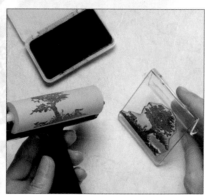

2 Ink the daydreamer stamp on the stained glass rainbow ink pad. Lay it down on the table and roll the brayer over the inked stamp to pick up the image on the brayer.

3 Roll the image on the brayer down on to the card, making sure that the base of the tree is in the centre and the tip of the tree is nearest to the offset end.

4 Turn the card through one hundred and eighty degrees and ink up the daydreamer stamp in the same area of the rainbow ink pad. Align the base of the stamp image with the brayed reflection image already on the card.

Tip

It is much easier to line up a clear stamp than a brayer, so position the brayer image on your card first, then the clear stamp.

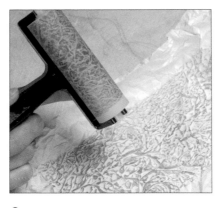

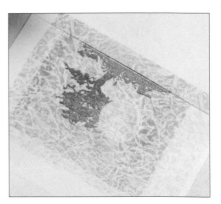

5 Draw two 2.5cm (1in) circles on a sticky note so there is an adhesive area on the back. Cut them out and place one on the right of the tree, and one on the right of the tree's reflection.

6 Crumple some scrap paper and unfurl it. Ink the brayer on the rainbow pad and roll it over the unfurled paper, creating a marbled effect on your brayer.

7 Place some scrap paper over the top half of the satin card, and roll the brayer once over the exposed half, making sure that the red ink is at the top of the water.

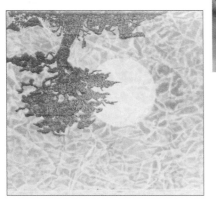

8 Remove the circle mask and lightly roll the brayer over the exposed half again to change the colour of the moon's reflection.

9 Remove the scrap paper and re-ink the brayer. Roll it across some scrap paper at an angle to remove some of the red ink, then roll it across the top half of the artwork, making sure that the faded part is at the bottom of the island. Remove the moon mask.

10 Ink the grass stamp in the green-blue area of the rainbow pad and stamp fairly randomly across the top edge of the picture so different parts of the stamp create a foliage effect.

11 Mirror the foliage effect at the bottom by blotting the stamp before pressing it on to the card.

12 Ink the moonshadow stamp across the red area of the ink pad, blot it and carefully stamp over the moon in the sky, looking through the stamp to get the placement correct.

13 Allow the ink to dry, then remove the masking tape. Use a craft knife and ruler to trim the card down so the picture has a 1cm (½in) border all round the edges.

14 Use the larger offcut of card to make a strip 2.5 x 11cm (1 x 4½in). Ink it with a marbled effect in the same way as the lake.

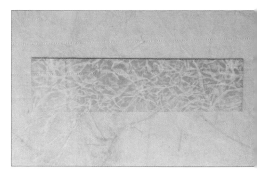

15 Make a dark blue card and attach the artwork and marbled strip with double-sided sticky tape to finish.

The Willow Lady

Using an alternative central stamp makes for a strikingly different finished piece.

The Ice Skater
Lightly sponging along the reflection line gives the illusion of ice instead of water.

Gone Fishing
The lad fishing is actually an addition to the landscape stamp. Use a brayer to place his reflection first, then stamp him in pace. You can then add the landscape around him.

Mail Art

I always have great fun creating faux postage stamps, and it is even more creative when you can stray beyond the box with a clear stamp as I have done here.

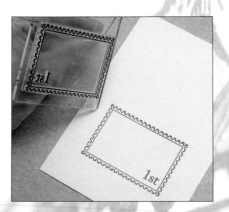

1 Cut your watercolour paper in half to get an A5 sheet, and stamp a large postage stamp towards the bottom with sepia ink.

2 Stamp a second identical postage stamp on scrap paper and use scissors to cut out the centre to make a large mask.

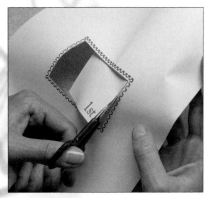

3 Use masking tape on the back to secure the mask in place over the watercolour paper. Use sepia ink with the la petite musique stamp to stamp over the hole as shown, making sure her elbow aligns with the top of the stamp.

4 Stamp la petite musique on a large sticky note, then cut around her silhouette with scissors. Cut out the space between her dress and hair to complete a detailed mask.

YOU WILL NEED

Clear stamps: large and small postage stamps, la petite musique

A4 orange textured card

A5 sheets of 300gsm (140lb) cold-pressed watercolour paper

Dye-based sepia archival ink pad

Dye-based plum ink pad

Dye-based cabin fever rainbow ink pad

Watercolour pencils: burnt ochre and burnt carmine

Large sticky yellow notes

Embroidery scissors

Decollage craft scissors

Make-up sponge

Brayer

Pencil

Paintbrush

Double-sided sticky tape

Scrap paper

Tip

For an authentic effect, always change the background colour of the postage stamp with a brayer or sponge – or both!

5 Place the small mask over the artwork and large mask. Use the brayer with the cabin fever rainbow ink pad, making sure you pick up red on the right-hand side of the brayer and yellow on the left-hand side. Remove some ink on scrap paper, then roll the brayer over the postage stamp area, making sure the red is at the bottom and the yellow at the top.

6 Pinch a make-up sponge into a mushroom shape and reinforce the colours at the bottom with the plum ink pad.

7 Make a mask of the large postage stamp on a sticky yellow note, taking care to cut around the serrated edge neatly. Remove the masks from the artwork and place the new mask on the artwork. Carefully trace the outline of la petite musique with the pencil.

8 Carefully stamp la petite musique in place over the new mask, using sepia ink.

9 Remove the new mask and use the burnt carmine watercolour pencil to colour her dress, and burnt ochre to colour her skin. Soften the colours with a damp brush.

10 Cut out a 5¾cm (2¼in) circle mask from a sticky yellow note and place it over her head. Replace the large postage stamp mask, then use a make-up sponge with the yellow part of the cabin fever ink pad to add colour around the mask.

11 Remove the masks and trim the artwork down to 11 x 13cm (4½ x 5¼in), using the craft scissors to get a distressed edge.

12 Use the small postage stamp with sepia ink on a 12 x 5cm (5 x 2in) strip of watercolour paper.

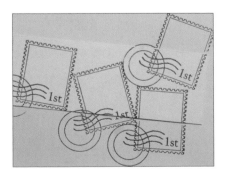

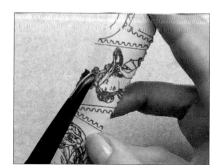

13 Add details inside the stamps with various parts of la petite musique and sepia ink.

14 Use the cabin fever rainbow ink pad with the brayer to add colour to the strip, then trim it to 10 x 2cm (4 x ¾in) with the decollage craft scissors.

Tip

Whenever you are using water or watercolour pencils, be sure to use a water-resistant archival ink pad to avoid the line art bleeding.

15 Use another sheet of watercolour paper to create mounts for the artwork and strip, then attach the mounted piece to an orange card with double-sided sticky tape.

Countryside Collage

To achieve an overlapped effect with the postage stamps, place the front three first. Next, mask the printed stamps off and stamp the next images into the background.

The large 'postage stamp' stamp is the same as I used for the demonstration. Note that the artwork is kept within the box here.

Friends and Lovers

Four independent faux postage stamps, to create a romantic mood. The panel incorporates all the stamps used in the individual images.

Two Tone

Here is a project that will test your eye for perfection. The cardstock you use will dictate the degree of success you have. I found using coated shiny card gave me the great embossed effect I was aiming for.

1 Cut a piece of white card to 6 x 13cm (2½ x 5½in). Use the cat stamp with the black ink pad to stamp the image into the centre.

2 Quickly pour clear embossing powder all over the wet ink and leave to dry.

YOU WILL NEED

Clear stamp: large cat back

A6 shiny white card

A5 black card

A5 red card

Dye-based black ink pad

Pigment white ink pad

White embossing powder

Clear embossing powder

Heat gun

7.5cm (3in) string of red beads

Decorative red brad

Double-sided sticky tape

Pencil

Paintbrush

Craft knife, cutting mat and metal-edged ruler

Tracing paper

Embroidery scissors

Needle

3 Pour the excess powder back into the pot, then heat the image from behind to melt the powder. This ensures the powder melts more slowly and does not get blown about, resulting in a finish as smooth as satin.

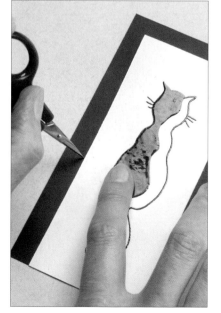

4 Cut a piece of black card to 8 x 15cm (3¼ x 6in). Place the artwork on top, aligning the bottom parts of both pieces of card. Use the point of your embroidery scissors to make two offset marks roughly halfway down the image on either side of the white card.

5 Remove the artwork and use a craft knife and the metal-edged ruler to cut a diagonal slit between the offset marks.

6 Cut a 6 x 13cm (2½ x 5½in) strip of tracing paper, lay it over the artwork and feed both through the slit.

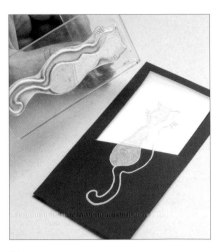

7 Use the cat stamp with white pigment ink and stamp the black card, using the part of the cat visible through the tracing paper as a guide.

8 Quickly remove the artwork and tracing paper and pour white embossing powder over the wet ink. Use a clean dry paintbrush to clear away excess embossing powder.

9 Use the heat tool to heat the powder from behind. Slot the artwork into the slit, line the parts of the cat up and secure the artwork in place with double-sided sticky tape.

10 Use embroidery scissors to prick two holes in the black card, one next to the top left corner of the visible artwork, the other next to the lower left corner of the visible artwork. Thread the string of beads on to a needle and take it through the top hole. Secure the thread on the back with masking tape (see inset).

11 Thread the other end on the needle and take it through the lower hole. Secure it on the back with tape.

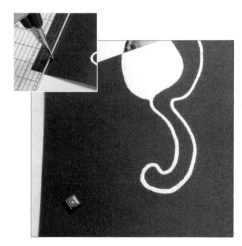

12 Make a hole in the bottom left of the black card with the point of the embroidery scissors, making sure it aligns with the row of beads by using a ruler (see inset). Place a decorative brad in the hole and secure it.

13 Mount the artwork on a piece of red card with double-sided sticky tape, then trim the red card down until it is only slightly bigger than the black. Attach the mounted piece to a white card using double-sided sticky tape.

Erté's Satin

The two red sprig panels are actually part of the same white postcard. By masking both sides and then cutting slits, the lower black-on-white section of the model slips behind the white-on-black piece, and the red sprig panels are then folded over the front and secured in place.

Three Reeds in a Row

This is probably the most challenging card in the book, but the thrill of completing a perfect card with not a speck of stray embossing powder is very rewarding.

Erté's Greek Velvet

An ornate corner jazzes up the white-on-black area, and some feathers add a splash of colour.

Grids

Grid cards are a joy to create, and the positioning of images is paramount so clear stamps are a must. There are a few basic guidelines: silhouette stamps work best; place the central image first and work outwards; try to avoid overlapping images, and use contrasting colours in neighbouring sections when shading.

YOU WILL NEED

Clear stamps: kissing, hanging vine, small grass, Eiffel tower, camelia, sprig, music score, dancer, piano, vine, fobwatch, Fifi, fern, snob, dippy-toe lady

A5 satin-finish white card

A4 orange card

A4 scrap paper

Brayer

Niagara mist chalk ink pad

Persimmon chalk ink pad

Dye-based black archival ink pad

Make-up sponge

Masking tape

Double-sided sticky tape

1 Use masking tape to make a frame round the satin-finish card, then use two more strips laid across at right angles to each other as shown.

2 Use the dippy-toe lady stamp with the black archival ink pad to stamp on a piece of scrap paper. Cut the image out and place it at the corner of the two extra strips of masking tape.

3 Lay another two strips of masking tape on the other sides of the mask.

4 Remove the mask, pinch a make-up sponge into a mushroom shape and use the Persimmon and Niagara mist inks to add areas of colour to the central section.

5 Use the dippy-toe lady stamp with black archival ink to stamp over the chalked area.

6 Remove all of the inner masking tape, then place two new strips to isolate the top right corner as shown.

7 Colour the area with the chalk ink pads, then use the kissing stamp with archival black ink to stamp an image.

8 Use parts of the hanging vine and small grass stamps to add interest to the top of the area.

9 Allow the ink to dry, remove the horizontal strip of tape and lay down two new strips to isolate the right-hand section as shown.

10 Colour with the chalk ink pads, then stamp the area with the Eiffel tower and camelia stamps. Use scrap paper to protect completed areas when using larger stamps.

11 Remove the horizontal masking tape once the ink is dry, then mask off the lower right corner and chalk it as before. Ink and blot the sprig stamp, then ink and use it unblotted over the top for a dense foliage effect.

12 Repeat the process on the lower central part, masking the area, chalking and stamping with the music score and dancer stamp.

13 Repeat the process with the piano and sprig stamps on the lower left area.

14 Use the vine and fobwatch stamps to complete the left-hand section.

15 Use the Fifi stamp, together with the fern stamp to complete the upper left section.

16 Complete the grid by using the snob and small grass stamps at the top, then remove all of the masking tape.

17 Mask off a narrow section on the right-hand side and decorate with the chalk ink pads.

18 Remove the masking tape and use the craft knife and ruler to trim the artwork to size, leaving a ½cm (¼in) border all round.

19 Mount the finished artwork on an orange card using double-sided tape.

Geisha in Red

*This variation uses just one colour in the background.
Here, the central image is not just a single stamp; it is
a miniature section just like the neighbouring areas.*

Africa

You can see here how independent sections can be randomly made to form a medley of African scenes.

Pinch an Inch

Independent fragments of Erté fashion images are built on each other to conjure a mood and a style. The measuring tape adds a subtle humorous twist.

Index

archival ink pad 7, 19, 20, 31, 33, 43, 44

background paper 8
beads 8, 13, 14, 15, 37, 38
border 13, 14, 16, 20
brads 8, 17, 19, 21, 37, 39
brayer 7, 25, 29, 31, 32, 33

card 6, 8, 10, 11, 13, 14, 15, 19, 21, 25, 27, 33, 37, 38, 39, 43
   coated (shiny) 8, 37
   textured 6, 13, 31
card blanks 8
chalk ink pad 7, 43, 44, 45
colouring pencil 13, 14
cord 13, 14
corner stamp 13, 14, 16, 17, 19, 20, 22, 41
craft scissors 9, 31, 33

dye-based ink 7, 8, 13

embellishments 8
embossed effect 37
embossing powder 9, 37, 38, 41

feathers 8, 41

gold leafing pen 9, 13, 15, 19, 20

heat gun 8, 37
hole punch 13, 14

mask 19, 26, 31, 32, 34
make-up sponges 9, 19, 20, 31, 32, 43
marble effect 26, 27
motif 15, 16

paintbrush 9, 19, 20, 31, 32, 33, 37, 38
pigment ink 8, 37, 38

rainbow ink pad 7, 22, 25, 26, 31, 32
reflection 25, 26, 29
repeating pattern 13
ribbon 8

scrap paper 13, 25, 26, 31, 32, 43, 44
sponge ink pad 7
sticky foam pads 13, 15
sticky yellow notes 13, 19, 20, 25, 26, 31, 32

textured paper 8, 13
tracing paper 37, 38

watercolour paper 13, 14, 15, 19, 31, 32, 33
watercolour pencils 31, 32, 33
wet wipe 9
wire 9, 13, 15

Kasha in the Shoe

An example of using one stamp (Kasha) to fill another (the shoe).

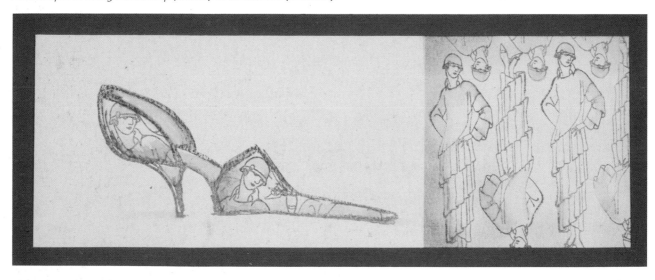